SECRET SQUID STORMS THE CASTLE

Illustrated by Barry Ablett

CONTENTS

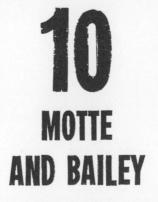

INTRODUCTION

Meet Secret Squid, a master of disguise who can be in a lot of different places at the same time! With a talent for hiding in plain sight, Squid is able to get into all kinds of mischief without being discovered.

SECRET MISSION

Secret Squid is on a sneaky mission to uncover the history of castles from around the world. Come along on a journey through time to see seven different fortresses and castles, as they would have looked in their heyday. Our tentacled friend is ready to take in the sights, make friends, and have bundles of fun!

Psst! All words in **bold** can be found in the glossary on page 40.

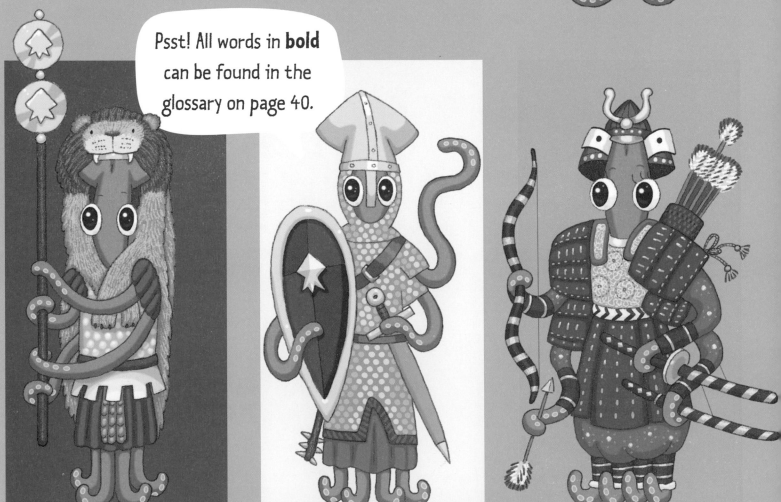

THE SEARCH IS ON

Can you find all of Secret Squid's hiding places? Our sneaky friend has snuck into 10 different locations in each scene, wearing some very clever disguises. While you are searching, don't forget to check out your surroundings. There is a lot to spot at each castle!

Having trouble finding me? All my hiding places are revealed on pages 38 – 39.

THE JOURNEY CONTINUES

Turn the page after each scene to discover more about each castle and what life was like for the people living within them.

ROMAN FORT

Roman forts were built at the borders of Rome's lands to protect their expanding **empire**. Inside their high defensive walls were various military buildings, housing hundreds of soldiers.

BARRACKS

This is where the soldiers slept. With eight to a room, it would have been a tight squeeze!

FORT WALLS

The first Roman forts were wooden but, by the second century CE, most were made from strong stone. The Romans invented an effective concrete mix, which has continued to hold some of their walls up for centuries!

ROMAN BATHS

Bathhouses were built outside of the main walls, so that sparks from the **furnace**, used to heat the water, would not burn down the fort.

STABLES

Horses were an important part of the Roman military. So much so, that their riders lived in the same building with them. This meant they could be quickly saddled at a moment's notice.

LATRINES

Cleanliness was very important to the Romans. Their latrines, which were toilets, had rows of seats positioned over a channel of running water to flush everything away. After doing their business, Romans would wash themselves with a sponge on a stick, which everyone shared. Yuck!

GRANARY

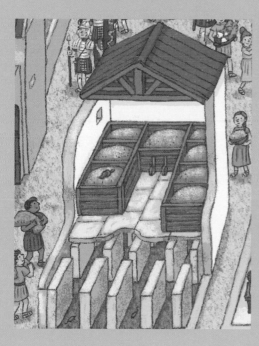

This is where grain used to make bread was stored. Raised floors stopped the grain from getting damp. The granary could store enough grain to feed the soldiers for six months, in case the fort came under **siege**.

PRINCIPIUM

The principium was the fort headquarters, where the commanding officer issued orders. It would have been well protected, because it was where they kept coins to pay the soliders!

AQUILIFER

The aquilifer, or eagle-bearer, would carry the eagle **standard** into battle. It was an important job, because the standard was the **Roman legion**'s most prized possession. The eagle was a symbol of power, and it represented courage, strength, and **immortality**.

MOTTE AND BAILEY

The Normans started building many of these castles across northern Europe in the tenth century. They were quick to build, but their wooden strutures could easily catch fire. Many were later replaced with stone castles.

PALISADE

The fence around the castle, called the palisade, was made from wooden logs with sharpened tips to prevent attackers from climbing over the top of them.

MOTTE

The motte was a tall mound with a flattened top, made by piling up soil. A deep ditch at the bottom and steep sides made it almost impossible to climb up without access to the bridge. This made the keep easy to defend.

BAILEY

Below the motte was a courtyard, called the bailey. It was surround by a palisade, and a ditch or **moat**, for defending purposes. Soldiers, servants, craftspeople, and animals lived there, and it contained various buildings, including kitchens, storerooms, stables, and workshops.

THE KEEP

The keep is the tower on top of the motte, where the lord of the land would live. Its high location made it the safest place to be, and you could spot any attackers coming from miles away!

BLACKSMITH

The bailey would have had a forge, where a blacksmith would have worked. They made and repaired metal weapons and equipment for the soldiers, as well as crafting horseshoes for the knights' horses.

FLYING BRIDGE

The motte and the bailey were sometimes connected by a wooden "flying bridge." If a battle was lost in the bailey, the soldiers would retreat to the motte, pulling up the bridge behind them to keep the attackers at bay.

NORMAN KNIGHTS

For protection in battle, a knight would wear a knee-length shirt made of **chain mail**, with slits that allowed them to sit on their horse. It was flexible and provided good protection, but it was very heavy!

WELL

A well was an important source of clean water for the castle, especially during a siege! To make a well, a hole was dug down into the ground until water was found. The walls were then lined with stone.

LIFE IN A MEDIEVAL CASTLE

Stone castles were first built in Europe in the late twelfth century. In times of peace, they would have hosted grand festivals and **tournaments** to show off the wealth and power of the lord of the castle.

JESTERS

Jesters were great entertainers who would perform songs, poems, and dances at feasts. They would also sometimes entertain soldiers before battle to raise their spirits.

JOUSTING

Jousting was a popular sport and was used to help keep knights prepared for battle. Knights needed to be skilled with all weapons, and were especially strong and fit.

CROSSBOWS

Crossbows became popular weapons in medieval Europe. They were slower to load and fire than a bow and arrow, but required less strength and skill to use. They were good for defending a castle and were powerful and accurate at close range.

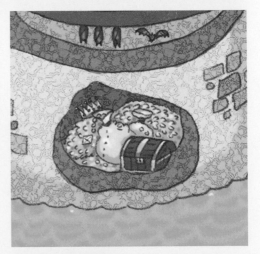

TREASURE

The castle's gold and treasure was closely guarded and kept in a place that was difficult for invaders to find.

CHESS

Chess is believed to have been invented in India. It came to Europe around the tenth century and became a popular game during medieval times.

TOILETS

These medieval toilets were called garderobes. They emptied straight into the moat. Since the water did not flow, it would have been very smelly!

THE GREAT HALL

The main room of the castle was the great hall. It was used by the lord and his family for feasting, entertaining guests, and as a place to conduct important business. **Tapestries** were often hung on the walls for decoration.

HONEY

Honey was used as a sweetener, a medicine, and to preserve food. It was highly valued and every castle kept their own hives.

MEDIEVAL CASTLE UNDER SIEGE

Sometimes an invading army or a rival noble lord would lay siege to a castle. Clever machines, known as **siege engines**, were used by the attackers to combat the castle's stronghold.

SIEGE TOWERS

These tall wooden towers would be wheeled up to the castle walls, loaded with soldiers, who would then try to climb over the **battlements**. Siege towers were sometimes covered in water-soaked animal hides to prevent them from catching fire.

FIRE ARROWS

Arrows dipped in oil and then set alight were used by both sides. Attackers would aim them over the castle walls to set fire to buildings, while defenders would fire them at the wooden siege engines.

SIEGE CAMP

Sieges sometimes lasted for months! With the castle surrounded, the attacking army would set up camp at a safe distance, and wait. With no one able to enter or leave the castle, there was a chance the people inside would eventually run out of food and be forced to surrender. However, in reality, this plan rarely worked.

MANTLETS

A mantlet was a large, portable shield or shelter used for protection by invading soldiers. Archers and crossbowmen would stand behind them and fire through holes in the middle.

BATTERING RAM

Battering rams were used to break down the gates and walls of a castle. The ram itself was usually a heavy wooden log with a metal tip. It was hung with ropes from a frame shaped like a roof, so that it could be swung against the wall or gate.

HELPFUL HOARDING

Hoards were temporary wooden structures that could be attached to the castle's battlements during a siege. Their platforms extended out from the castle walls, improving the range of fire and letting defenders aim directly below them at attackers close to the wall.

TREBUCHETS

One of the most powerful siege engines, trebuchets were a type of long-armed catapult, used to throw heavy rocks and other **missiles** at, and over, castle walls.

BALLISTA

Ballistas were like giant crossbows, used to fire large **bolts** or rocks at the castle walls to cause damage to them. The first ballistas were developed by the ancient Greeks.

JAPANESE CASTLE

This style of castle started to develop around the sixteenth century. The base was made of stone, but most of the buildings were wooden. The grounds were designed to confuse and trap invaders in a complicated maze of pathways, walls, and courtyards.

NINJAS

Ninja means "those who act with stealth." They were used as secret agents, spies and **assassins**. They wore dark clothing, to help them blend into the shadows, and were skilled in **martial arts**.

STONE DROP WINDOWS

Ishi-otoshi windows had holes for throwing stones or boiling liquid down onto attackers below.

SIEGE ENGINES

The Japanese would use siege engines, similar to the Europeans, to lay siege to castles from the outside.

DEFENSIVE DEVICE

The gruesome "wolf's tooth" device was dropped down onto attackers who tried to scale the walls.

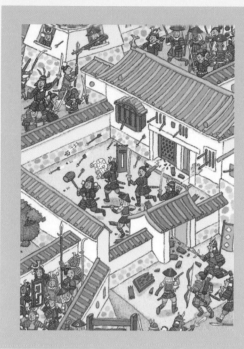

A CLEVER TRAP

A *masugata* was a special gateway designed to trick attackers. It included two gates, separated by a small rectangular space, where defensive troops would lie in wait. Attackers who made it through the first gate would have a horrible surprise waiting for them!

LADDERS

Wooden scaling ladders were used to reach the top of the walls to gain access to the interior of the castle.

SAMURAI

Samurai were powerful, highly skilled warriors, who came from noble families. They ruled Japan from 1185–1868. They followed a strict code of conduct, called *Bushido*, meaning "way of the warrior," to be respectful, loyal, and self-disciplined. As well as male warriors, some samurai women were also trained to fight.

TANEGASHAMI GUNS

These guns were introduced to Japan by the Portuguese in 1543. They dramatically changed how the Japanese fought wars, and even affected the design of future castles.

BASTION FORT

Medieval castle walls were no match for powerful cannons! The invention of gunpowder led to a new design of fortress, known as bastion or star forts. The first examples were found in Italy in the middle of the fifteenth century.

THE WALLS

The walls of a bastion fort were sloped, angular, and much lower than medieval towers, making them harder to topple. They were usually made from packed earth and brick, which could absorb the impact of cannonballs much better than stone.

HIGH SOCIETY

Many bastion forts were designed purely for military reasons, but a few, such as Kronborg in Denmark, contained palaces for royalty or nobles.

BASTIONS

Bastions were the outer, angular defensive sections of the fortress, which were often arranged in the shape of a star. Their shape gave the gunners a much wider view to fire their cannons on attackers, leaving nowhere for them to hide.

A LOSING BATTLE

The clever design of these forts put a temporary end to naval sieges. Sinkable, wooden ships were no match for the bastions' strong defensive structure.

FIGUREHEAD

Figureheads are the carved wooden sculptures that decorate the **prow** of a ship. Some sailors believed they would offer them protection from stormy seas.

MUSKETEERS

A musketeer was a soldier who carried a musket, a type of gun often used in the sixteenth and seventeenth centuries. Muskets were heavy, so portable rests were sometimes used to hold the barrel of the gun still while taking aim.

CANNONS

From the thirteenth century, cannons began replacing siege weapons, such as the trebuchet. They worked by using explosive gunpowder to fire heavy cannonballs out of the cannon's barrel with great force. Each shot could travel long distances and do serious damage!

WARSHIPS

From the sixteenth century, warships were equipped with rows of cannons on both sides of the **hull**. Using them was hard work! The highly flammable gunpowder was kept in storage areas below deck for safety. Powder boys, as young as 10 years old, would have had to run back and forth, carrying it up to the cannons.

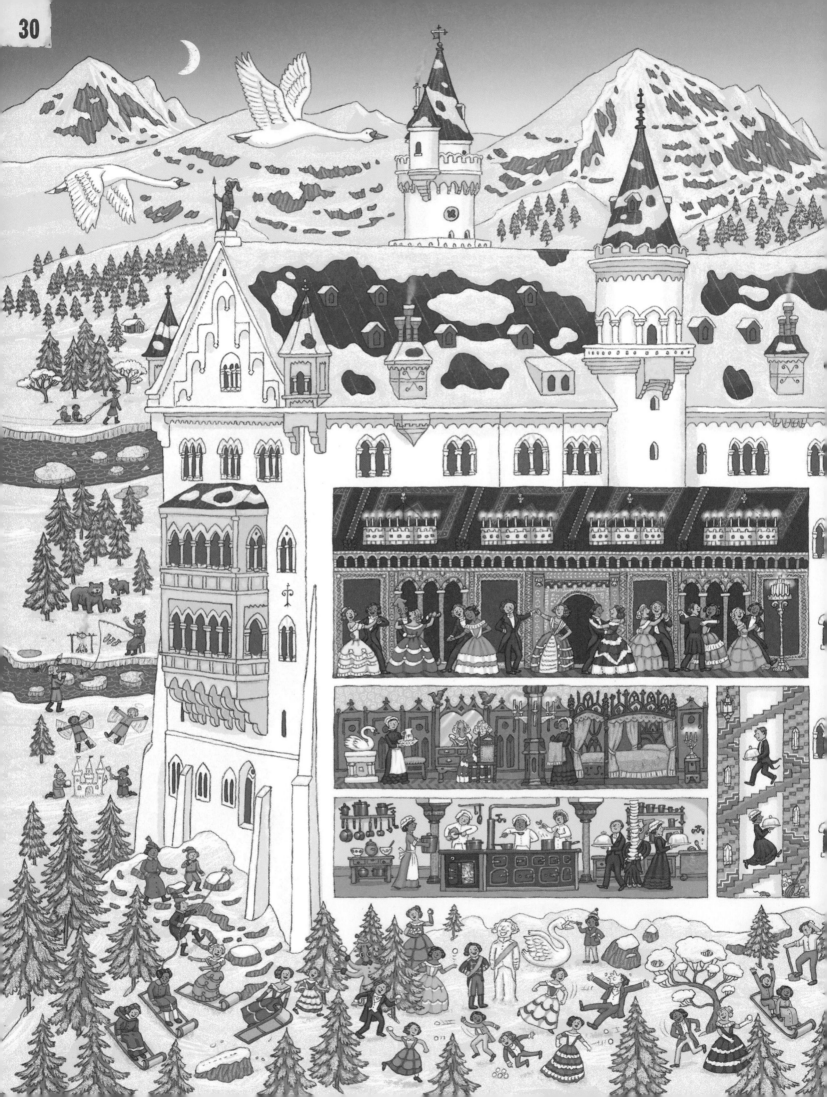

19TH-CENTURY CASTLE

By the nineteenth century, defensive castles had long been a thing of the past. Instead, the nobility built grand palaces and mansions to live in. Some still looked like castles, but they would not have been much use against an invading army!

GRAND BALLS

Balls were large formal dance parties. They were grand events, which often included a banquet. Palaces would contain ballrooms designed just to host these dances.

THE REAL CASTLE

The castle in this scene is based on Neuschwanstein Castle in Germany. It was built for King Ludwig II of Bavaria as a retreat, but it was never fully completed. It is the ultimate fairy-tale castle and was one of the inspirations for Walt Disney's Cinderella castle.

INSPIRED BY THE PAST

In nineteenth-century Europe, people began to feel **nostalgia** for the medieval era. Many buildings of the time were greatly inspired by medieval architecture. Grand houses and palaces would often include traditional castle features, such as towers and **turrets**, but these were for decoration instead of for protection.

SIMPLE LIVING

Servant's bedrooms were small and plain compared to the other grand rooms in the palace, and they would often have had to share.

UPSTAIRS, DOWNSTAIRS

Palaces like this would have had a lot of servants working in them. Most of them were not meant to be seen by the owners or their guests, so they had separate entrances and staircases. Servant's rooms were found on the lowest floors of the palace.

KITCHENS

Grand palaces and castles would have had large kitchens, where cooks and servants would have prepared elaborate banquets.

FUN IN THE SNOW

Winter sports, such as ice skating and sledding, were popular pastimes for men, women, and children.

FAIRY TALES

Fairy tales became popular in the nineteenth century, when people, such as the Brothers Grimm, started to collect and write down traditional folk tales. These included stories that are still popular today, such as Rapunzel and Little Red Riding Hood.

DID YOU SPOT...

Here are some interesting castle features and items that you may have missed. Head back through the book to see if you can find them all.

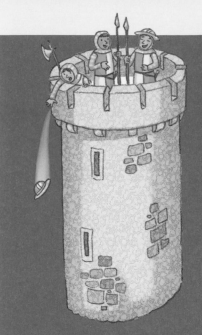

...SLANTED WALLS

Some castles had slanted walls that were wider at the bottom. These were often more resistant to attack from siege engines. They also made it more difficult to use ladders to climb over them.

Find on pages 22–23

...WATCHTOWERS

Watchtowers have been an important part of fortresses and castles since ancient times. They were used as lookout points to spot approaching enemies.

Find on pages 14–15

...BUCKETS OF HOT WATER

A lot of movies show people pouring hot oil onto the attackers below. Historians believe this did not happen, because oil was expensive. It was probably boiling water, which is still not pleasant!

Find on pages 18–19

...SHIELDS

Depending on the time and place, shields came in different shapes and sizes. They were designed to protect soldiers in combat. Shields were often painted with bright designs to make it clear what side the wearer was fighting for, like football uniforms today!

SCUTUM

This shield was used by the Romans from about the fourth century BCE. Its curved, rectangular shape allowed for soldiers to overlap their shields to create a protective wall all around them. This was known as a "tortoise formation," because it looked like a shell.

Find on pages 6–7

KITE SHIELD

This style of shield was used by the Normans. Its shape was designed for use on horseback. The narrowed base would fit well against the horse's neck and protect the rider's leg.

Find on pages 10–11

HEATER SHIELD

These shields were popular in Europe between the twelfth and fifteenth centuries. They were lighter and easier to handle than the kite shield but offered less protection for the legs. They were made from thin wood covered with leather or thin metal.

Find on pages 14–15

...FLAGS

Samurai would wear flags and banners into battle as a kind of uniform, so they could be easily identified. They would often be attached to their backs so that they could still use both arms to fight.

Find on pages 22–23

...CATAPULT

Catapults were a type of siege engine first used in ancient Rome. It worked by tightly winding a rope at the base of the throwing arm, creating a spring effect when released, like a giant slingshot.

Find on pages 18–19

SHACHIHOKU

The *shachihoku* was a mythical animal from Japanese folklore, with the head of a tiger and the body of a carp. It was believed that they could control the rain, so sculptures of them were often attached to the roofs of castles and temples to protect them from fire.

Find on pages 22–23

...DRAWBRIDGES

A drawbridge was a strong wooden bridge that reached across a moat or trench. It could be raised and lowered to let people in, or keep them out!

Find on pages 10–11

...TRENCHES

Trenches were often dug around castles and fortresses as a way to stop attackers reaching the castle walls. They often had spikes or other obstacles within them. Trenches could also be filled with water to create a moat.

Find on pages 10–11

...CRENELLATED WALLS

You often see this shape of battlement on city walls and castles. The gaps allowed soldiers to shoot through the openings at attackers while remaining mostly protected from any incoming fire.

Find on pages 14–15

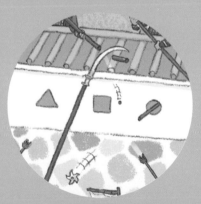

...COATS OF ARMS

Lords and knights would often have their own coat of arms, which was a uniquely decorated shield. They often became the symbol of their house or family and were used to decorate great halls.

Find on pages 14–15

...THROWING STARS

Shuriken, known as throwing stars, were a type of throwing dagger used by ninjas and samurai. Although they were small and easy to conceal, they could do a lot of damage! The blades were also sometimes coated with poison.

Find on pages 22–23

...LOOP HOLES

Arrow slits and loop holes were small holes in a castle's walls. Archers—and later gunmen—could fire through them while staying protected behind the wall. They came in different shapes.

Find on pages 22–23

ANSWERS

Did you manage to find all of Secret Squid's hiding places?

ROMAN FORT Pages 6–7

MOTTE AND BAILEY Pages 10–11

LIFE IN A MEDIEVAL CASTLE
Pages 14–15

MEDIEVAL CASTLE UNDER SIEGE
Pages 18–19

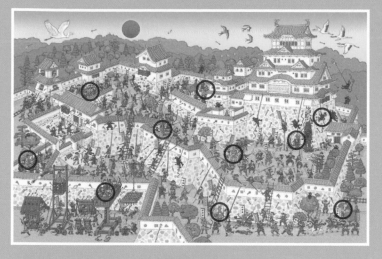

JAPANESE CASTLE Pages 22-23

BASTION FORT Pages 26-27

19TH-CENTURY CASTLE
Pages 30-31

Check the circles on these pictures to reveal my secret locations.

GLOSSARY

assassins—People who murder important people, usually for political or religious reasons, but also for money.

bolts—A short, heavy type of arrow, fired from a crossbow or ballista.

chain mail—A protective metal fabric made from small metal rings joined together to look like cloth.

empire—A collection of lands or regions ruled by a single ruler or state.

furnace—An enclosed chamber where heat is produced.

hull—The main body of a ship.

immortality—The ability to live forever.

martial arts—Any of several styles of physical combat, originally developed in East Asia, including karate and judo.

missiles—An object that is thrown with the intention of causing injury or damage.

moat—A deep, wide ditch surrounding a castle, fort, or town, which is filled with water to defend them.

nostalgia—A feeling of longing for, or desire to return to, a time in the past.

prow—The pointed front of a ship.

Roman legion—The largest type of military unit in the Roman army.

siege—The act of surrounding a place by armed forces, in an attempt to defeat the people defending it.

siege engine—Large weapons used during a siege to break through the walls and gates of a castle, fortress, or city.

standard—An object, such as a banner or statue, carried into battle on top of a pole. It was a symbol of pride and encouragement to the army, and was also a way to communicate in battle.

tapestries—Thick fabric with decorative pictures woven into them, often used as wall hangings.

tournaments—Sporting events or competitions. A medieval tournament would consist of multiple events, including jousting and sword fighting, where knights would compete against each other.

turrets—Small towers that extend out from the wall of a building, such as a castle.

First published in 2023 by Hungry Tomato Ltd.
F15, Old Bakery Studios, Blewetts Wharf, Malpas Road, Truro, Cornwall, TR1 1QH, UK

Thanks to our creative team
Senior Editor: Anna Hussey
Graphic Designer: Amy Harvey

Historical Consultant: John Haywood

Beetle Books is an imprint of Hungry Tomato.

ISBN 978-1-914087-76-9

Printed and bound in China.

A CIP catalog record for this book is available from the British Library.

Discover more at:
www.mybeetlebooks.com
www.hungrytomato.com